Contents

Other books in this series

Previously published...
- Maths and Calculator skills for Science Students   March 2016
- Maths (The Chemistry bits) for GCSE Combined Science   May 2016
- Maths (The Chemistry bits) for GCSE Triple Science   May 2016
- Science revision Guide   April 2017
- Maths Revision Guide   April 2017
- Summer Start for A-Level Chemistry   May 2017

Coming soon...
- Atoms, Electrons, Structure and Bonding Workbook
- Organic Chemistry Workbook
- Maths (The Physics bits) for GCSE Combined Science
- Maths (The Physics bits) for GCSE Triple Science
- Summer Start for A-Level Physics
- Maths for A-Level Chemistry

Chances are if you want a maths/science book I've written it or I am writing it.

For full book listings visit www.PrimroseKitten.com

First published 2017

Copyright; Primrose Kitten ©

Image credits, pixabay

Acknowledgements

Thank you to my husband for putting up with my spending every night writing this and for correcting all of my SPG mistakes. To my sons for being the inspiration behind Primrose Kitten. To Aimee for kick-starting this book. ☺

Introduction

Welcome to this workbook and thank you for supporting me to make more videos by buying this. ☺

I'm constantly telling you the best way to learn is by practising questions, so I've made you a book full of practice questions.

135 multiple choice questions to reflect the style of exam questions, 60 equations for you to balance (in 3 different formats), 65 compounds for you to work out the formula for and a lots of things that you need to recall for A-Level.

This book is not designed as a text book or revision guide, but as a workbook. There are lots of good (and bad) expensive and free revision guides out there, on my YouTube channel and other great websites. So there is no point in me adding to the masses.

Taking some GCSE topics, a bit further and introducing some new topics for A-Level. This is not a complete list of all the GCSE topics that also come up at A-Level; just enough to keep you (Very) busy over the summer and give you an advantage when you start year 12.

All the teaching, all the new content, is available for free on my YouTube channel, this book is for you to practice and learn. The best way to approach this is to watch the teaching video, or after class try a section and check the answers.

All the videos mentioned in this workbook are collected together in this playlist
https://www.youtube.com/playlist?list=PL7O6CcKg0HaEXpTtPXEiOfcZFsmhdle6e

Atomic Structure

Video links; The Atom, Isotopes and Ions - Atoms, Electrons, Structure and Bonding #1
https://youtu.be/POTn3f4O-iE

1. Which element has 2 protons?

   Helium ✓

   a. Hydrogen
   b. Helium
   c. Lithium
   d. Neon

2. Which element has 7 protons?

   Nitrogen ✓

   a. Nitrogen
   b. Lithium
   c. Carbon
   d. Helium

3. Which element has 31 protons?

   Gallium ✓

   a. Gallium
   b. Sodium
   c. Phosphorus
   d. Vanadium

4. Which element has 24 protons?

   Chromium ✓

   a. Chromium
   b. Cobalt
   c. Magnesium
   d. Gallium

5. Which element has an atomic number of 38?

   Strontium ✓

   a. Potassium
   b. Strontium
   c. Calcium
   d. Rubidium

6. Which element has an atomic number of 20?

   Calcium ✓

   a. Neon
   b. Calcium
   c. Potassium
   d. Argon

7. Which element has an atomic number of 11?

Sodium ✓

a. Boron
b. Lithium
c. Sodium
d. Helium

8. Which element has an atomic number of 12?

Magnesium ✓

a. Magnesium
b. Carbon
c. Fluorine
d. Silicon

9. Which element has an atomic number of 14?

Silicon ✓

a. Carbon
b. Nitrogen
c. Silicon
d. Fluorine

10. Which element has a mass number of 14?

Nitrogen ✓

a. Carbon
b. Nitrogen
c. Silicon
d. Fluorine

11. Which element has a mass number of 12?

Carbon ✓

a. Magnesium
b. Carbon
c. Fluorine
d. Silicon

12. Which element has a mass number of 11?

Boron ✓

a. Boron
b. Lithium
c. Sodium
d. Helium

13. Which element has a mass number of 40?

Potassium ✗ *Argon*
   • Mistake

a. Zirconium
b. Scandium
c. Potassium
d. Argon

14. Which element has 3 electrons?

Lithium ✓

a. Hydrogen
b. Helium
c. Lithium
d. Neon

15. Which element has 10 electrons?

Neon ✓

    a. Neon
    b. Calcium
    c. Potassium
    d. Argon

16. Which element has 19 electrons?

Potassium ✓

    a. Neon
    b. Calcium
    c. Potassium
    d. Argon

17. Which element has 8 neutrons?

Oxygen ✓

    a. Oxygen
    b. Sodium
    c. Phosphorus
    d. Vanadium

18. Which element has 12 neutrons?

Sodium ✓

    a. Oxygen
    b. Sodium
    c. Phosphorus
    d. Magnesium

19. Which element has 35 neutrons?

Zinc ✓

    a. Cobalt
    b. Zinc
    c. Arsenic
    d. Yttrium

20. Which element has 50 neutrons?

Yttrium ✓

    a. Cobalt
    b. Zinc
    c. Arsenic
    d. Yttrium

19/20

Properties of Ionic Compounds

Video links;

Drawing Ionic Bonding - Atoms, Electrons, Structure and Bonding #3
https://youtu.be/pvaQMCkuGLE

Properties of ionic compounds - Atoms, Electrons, Structure and Bonding #4
https://youtu.be/_h4mVHBANAA

1. Which of the following are likely to show ionic bonding?

a. HCl ✗
b. NaCl ✓
c. Na
d. Cl_2

$$\left[Na \right]^{+} \left[\begin{matrix} & \text{xx} & \\ ^{o}_{x} & Cl & ^{x}_{x} \\ & \text{xx} & \end{matrix} \right]^{-}$$

2. Which of the following are likely to show ionic bonding?

a. H_2SO_4
b. Fe
c. MgO ✓
d. CO

$$\left[Mg \right]^{2+} \left[\begin{matrix} & \text{xx} & \\ ^{\bullet}_{\bullet} & O & ^{x}_{x} \\ & \text{xx} & \end{matrix} \right]^{2-}$$

3. Which of the following are likely to show ionic bonding?

a. I_2
b. K
c. KI ✓
d. HI

4. Which of the following are properties of ionic compounds

high m.p.
high b.p.

a. High melting point high boiling point and always conducts electricity
b. Low melting point low boiling point and always conducts electricity
c. High melting point high boiling point and conducts when molten or dissolved ✓   ↳ charged particles free to move.
d. Low melting point low boiling point and conducts when molten or dissolved

5. Why do ionic compounds conduct when molten or dissolved?

a. They always conduct electricity no matter what the state.
b. The positive ions need to be able to give up electrons
c. They don't
d. Free movement of ions ✓

6. What happens to electrons in ionic bonding?

a. Nothing
b. Shared ✓✗
c. Disappears
d. Transferred ✓

7. Which of the following pair of statements about charges is true?

a. Both metals and non-metals will be positive
b. Both metals and non-metals will be negative
c. Metals will be positive and non-metals will be negative ✓✓
d. Metals will be negative and non-metals will be positive

8. What charge will a sodium ion have?

a. 0
b. +1 ✓✓
c. -1
d. +2

9. What charge will a calcium ion have?

a. 0
b. +1
c. -1
d. +2 ✓✓

10. What charge will a chlorine ion have?

a. 0
b. +1
c. -1 ✓✓
d. +2

11. a negative ion is attracted to …

a. only the positive ion that donated an electron
b. only the closest positive ion to it
c. any positive ion that is close enough to feel an attraction ✓✓
d. all positive ions in the lattice

12. an ionic bond is…

a. one atom donating an electron to another atom
b. an electrostatic attraction between two neighbouring ions ✓✗
c. an electrostatic attraction between any neighbouring ions ✓
d. two atoms sharing electrons

13. ionic compounds are soluble in water because…

a. water wiggles in-between ions
b. the slight charges on water break down the lattice ✓✓
c. everything is soluble in water
d. they are not soluble in water

14. ionic compounds are soluble in…

a. only non-polar solvents ✓ ✗
b. any solvent
c. only polar solvents ✓
d. any solvent at high enough temperatures

15. a giant ionic lattice is made up of…

a. groups of molecules
b. a large network of paired ions
c. only giant ions, smaller ions don't form a lattice
d. ions that are strongly bonded to all neighbouring ions ✓ ✓

12/15

Simple Covalent Bonding

Video links;

Drawing Covalent Bonding Lewis Structures or Dot and Cross-Atoms, Electrons, Structure and Bonding#6 https://youtu.be/4SkHncOprhs

Properties of simple covalent compounds - Atoms, Electrons, Structure and Bonding #7 https://youtu.be/2-CjI8nWFW0

Dative Coordinate Covalent Bonding - Atoms, Electrons, Structure and Bonding #8 https://youtu.be/2sRU6KbL3sE

1. Which pair of elements is going to form a covalent bond?
   a. magnesium and iodine
   b. aluminium and oxygen
   c. fluorine and sulfur
   d. sodium and iron

2. Which pair of elements is going to form a covalent bond?
   a. lithium and chlorine
   b. hydrogen and oxygen
   c. calcium and carbon
   d. aluminium and nitrogen

3. Which pair of elements is most likely to form a covalent bond?
   a. carbon and chlorine
   b. carbon and iron
   c. carbon and neon
   d. carbon and magnesium

4. Which of these compounds show covalent bonding?
   a. $AlCl_3$
   b. PCl_3
   c. Al_2O_3
   d. Li_2O

5. Which of these compounds show covalent bonding?
   a. MgO
   b. $CHCl_3$
   c. BeF_2
   d. $NaOH$

6. Which of the following reasons explains the low melting point of covalent substances?

a. Weak intramolecular forces within the molecules
b. The free electrons between the atoms creates weak bonding
c. The metals create uneven bonding with the non-metals
d. Weak intermolecular forces between the molecules.

7. Which set of properties are true for covalent compounds

a. low melting point, low boiling point and conducts electricity
b. low melting point, high boiling point and doesn't conduct electricity
c. low melting point, high boiling point and conducts electricity
d. low melting point, low boiling point and doesn't conduct electricity

8. How many electrons are shared by each element in a single covalent bond?

a. 1
b. 2
c. 3
d. 4

9. How many electrons are shared by each element in a double covalent bond?

a. 1
b. 2
c. 3
d. 4

10. How many electrons are shared by each element in a dative covalent bond?

a. 1 and 1
b. 2 and 2
c. 2 and 0
d. 2 and 1

11. Which of the following have only single bonds?

a. CO_2
b. CO
c. Cl_2
d. N_2

12. Which of the following have only double bonds?

a. CO_2
b. CO
c. Cl_2
d. N_2

13. Which of the following have only triple bonds?

a. CO_2
b. CO
c. Cl_2
d. N_2

14. Which of the following is going to show dative covalent bonding?

a. NH_3
b. NH_4^+
c. H_2O
d. CH_4

15. Which of the following is going to show dative covalent bonding?

a. NH_3BF_3
b. PF_3
c. H_2SO_4
d. $CaCO_3$

16. Which of the following is going to show dative covalent bonding?

a. CO
b. CO_2
c. CH_4
d. $NaOH$

17. What type of bonds are in O_2?

a. Single
b. Double
c. Triple
d. Dative

18. What type of bonds are in HF?

a. Single
b. Double
c. Triple
d. Dative

19. What type of bonds are in pentane?

a. Single
b. Double
c. Triple
d. Dative

20. What type of bonds are in CN^-

a. Single
b. Double
c. Triple
d. Dative

Reference table of common ions formulae

YOU NEED TO LEARN ALL OF THESE!!!

I don't like to shout but it's really important, readymade flashcards are available from my website to help

As a general rule; elements in group one form +1 ions, group 2 +2 ions, group 6 -2 ions and group 7 -1 ions.

The roman numerals in brackets refer to the oxidation state. Oxidation states are explained a bit later on.

Positive		Negative	
Hydrogen	H^+	Fluoride	F^-
Lithium	Li^+	Chloride	Cl^-
Sodium	Na^+	Bromide	Br^-
Potassium	K^+	Iodide	I^-
Copper (I)	Cu^+	Hydroxide	OH^-
Silver	Ag^+	Nitrate	NO_3^-
Ammonium	NH_4^+	Nitrite	NO_2^-
		Hydrogencarbonate	HCO_3^-
Magnesium	Mg^{2+}	Hydrogensulfate	HSO_4^-
Barium	Ba^{2+}		
Strontium	Sr^{2+}	Sulfate	SO_4^{2-}
Calcium	Ca^{2+}	Carbonate	CO_3^{2-}
Iron (II)	Fe^{2+}	Sulfide	S^{2-}
Copper (II)	Cu^{2+}	Oxide	O^{2-}
Nickel (II)	Ni^{2+}		
Zinc	Zn^{2+}	Nitride	N^{3-}
Tin (II)	Sn^{2+}	phosphate	PO_4^{3-}
Lead (II)	Pb^{2+}		
Chromium	Cr^{3+}		
Iron (III)	Fe^{3+}		
Aluminium	Al^{3+}		

Formula of Ionic Compounds

Video links;

Formula of Ionic Compounds - Atoms, Electrons, Structure and Bonding #5
https://youtu.be/ipz1UMP1YYY

For each of these give the formula

1. silver iodide
2. magnesium iodine
3. lithium iodide
4. lead (II) iodide
5. copper (II) iodide
6. iron (III) bromide
7. iron (II) bromide
8. barium bromide
9. strontium bromide
10. strontium chloride
11. copper (II) chloride
12. iron (II) chloride
13. calcium chloride
14. lithium chloride
15. barium chloride
16. sodium oxide
17. potassium oxide
18. zinc oxide
19. aluminium oxide
20. strontium oxide
21. copper (I) oxide
22. copper (II) oxide
23. iron (III) oxide
24. iron (II) oxide
25. chromium (III) oxide
26. iron (II) carbonate
27. ammonium carbonate
28. copper (II) carbonate
29. lead (II) carbonate

30. sodium carbonate

31. magnesium carbonate

32. iron (II) carbonate

33. barium carbonate

34. potassium hydrogencarbonate

35. strontium hydrogencarbonate

36. lithium hydrogencarbonate

37. ammonium hydrogencarbonate

38. sodium hydrogencarbonate

39. magnesium hydrogencarbonate

40. ammonium sulfide

41. iron (II) sulfide

42. aluminium sulfide

43. iron (III) sulfate

44. iron (II) sulfate

45. lead (II) sulfate

46. aluminium sulfate

47. zinc sulfate

48. barium sulfate

49. ammonium sulfate

50. magnesium sulfate

51. lithium sulfate

52. magnesium hydroxide

53. aluminium hydroxide

54. potassium hydroxide

55. ammonium hydroxide

56. barium hydroxide

57. lithium hydroxide

58. calcium hydroxide

59. strontium hydroxide

60. aluminium nitrate

61. ammonium nitrate

62. lead (II) nitrate

63. sodium nitrite

64. lithium nitride

65. magnesium nitride

Oxidation Numbers

Video links;

The Rules - Oxidation States - Atoms, Electrons, Structure and Bonding #12
https://youtu.be/DlLY8nJlwgE

Naming Compound Using Oxidation States - Atoms, Electrons, Structure and Bonding #13
https://youtu.be/Nr4hZYGjmOA

Formula of Compounds Using Oxidation States - Atoms, Electrons, Structure and Bonding #14
https://youtu.be/GFYvIliJheI

Redox Reactions and Oxidation States - Atoms, Electrons, Structure and Bonding #15
https://youtu.be/OLPhqYrMoWI

Exceptions to the Rules of Oxidation States - Atoms, Electrons, Structure and Bonding #16
https://youtu.be/1gxLloqM8Sg

Disproportionation Redox Reactions and Oxidation States-Atoms, Electrons, Structure and Bonding
#17 https://youtu.be/59Dn63BEDMA

The Rules

-all uncombined elements have an oxidation state of 0
-molecules with only one element in have an oxidation state of 0
-the oxidation state of an ion is the same as its charge.
-in a compound the sum of the oxidation states is equal to the overall oxidation state.
-oxygen nearly always has an oxidation state of -2, except when combined with fluorine or a peroxide.
-hydrogen in nearly always +1, except when combined as a hydride when it is -1.
-fluorine is always -1.
-chlorine is nearly always -1, except when combined with fluorine or oxygen

1. What is the oxidation state of Br in Br_2?

a. 0
b. +2
c. -2
d. +1

2. What is the oxidation state of H^+?

a. 0
b. +1
c. -1
d. 1

3. What is the oxidation state of C in CO_2?

a. +4
b. +2
c. -2
d. -4

4. What is the oxidation state of F in SF_6?

a. -1
b. +6
c. +1
d. -6

5. What is the oxidation state of P in PO_4^{3-}?

a. +11
b. +8
c. +5
d. +3

6. In the following reaction state which element has been oxidised.

$$2Fe + 3Cl_2 \rightarrow 2FeCl_3$$

a. both
b. neither
c. iron
d. chlorine

7. In the following reaction state which element has been oxidised.

$$H_2 + Cl_2 \rightarrow 2HCl$$

a. both
b. neither
c. hydrogen
d. chlorine

8. In the following reaction state which element has been oxidised.

$$2FeCl_2 + Cl_2 \rightarrow 2FeCl_3$$

a. both
b. neither
c. iron
d. chlorine

9. In the following reaction state which element has been oxidised.
$$2H_2O + 2F_2 \rightarrow 4HF + O_2$$

a. none of them
b. fluorine
c. hydrogen
d. oxygen

10. In the following reaction state which element has been oxidised.
$$Cl_2 + 2I^- \rightarrow 2Cl^- + I_2$$

a. both
b. neither
c. chlorine
d. iodine

11. Give the full name for SnO

a. tin oxide
b. tin oxide (II)
c. tin(II) oxide
d. tin(IV) oxide

12. Give the full name for SnO_2

a. tin oxide
b. tin oxide (II)
c. tin(II) oxide
d. tin(IV) oxide

13. Give the full name for $PbCl_4$

a. lead chloride (IV)
b. lead(IV) chloride
c. lead(IV) chloride (IV)
d. lead(I) chloride

14. Give the full name for $Mn(OH)_2$

a. manganese(II) hydroxide
b. manganese hydroxide (II)
c. manganese(I) hydroxide
d. manganese(II) hydroxide (II)

15. Give the full name for Cu_2O

a. copper(I) oxide
b. copper(II) oxide
c. copper(III) oxide
d. copper(IV) oxide

16. Write the formula for copper (II) nitrate (V)

a. $Cu_2(NO_3)_5$
b. $CuNO_3$
c. $Cu(NO_3)_2$
d. Cu_2NO_5

17. Write the formula for potassium chlorate (III)

a. KCl_2
b. $KClO_2$
c. KCl_3
d. $KClO_3$

18. Write the formula for iron (III) hydroxide

a. Fe_3OH
b. $Fe_3(OH)_3$
c. $Fe(OH)_3$
d. $Fe_2(OH)_2$

19. Write the formula for sodium chlorate (v)

a. $NaCl_5$
b. $NaCl_3$
c. $NaClO_5$
d. $NaClO_3$

20. Write the formula for chromium(III) oxide

a. Cr_2O_3
b. Cr_3O_2
c. Cr_3O
d. Cr_3O_3

Balancing Equations 1

These are best done by trial and error

Video links; https://youtu.be/HxKOigOcJD8

1. $Mg + HIO_3 \rightarrow Mg(IO_3) + H_2$ $2Mg + 2HIO_3 \rightarrow 2Mg(IO_3) + H_2$ ✓
2. $BaCl_2 + Na_2SO_4 \rightarrow NaCl + BaSO_4$ $BaCl_2 + Na_2SO_4 \rightarrow 2NaCl + BaSO_4$ ✓
3. $NaI + HOCl \rightarrow NaIO_3 + HCl$ $NaI + 3HOCl \rightarrow NaIO_3 + 3HCl$ ✓
4. $Al + MnO_2 \rightarrow Al_2O_3 + Mn$ $4Al + 3MnO_2 \rightarrow 2Al_2O_3 + 3Mn$ ✓
5. $Ba(OH)_2 + H_2SO_4 \rightarrow BaSO_4 + H_2O$ $Ba(OH)_2 + H_2SO_4 \rightarrow BaSO_4 + 2H_2O$ ✓
6. $K_2CO_3 + AgNO_3 \rightarrow KNO_3 + Ag_2CO_3$ $K_2CO_3 + 2AgNO_3 \rightarrow 2KNO_3 + Ag_2CO_3$ ✓
7. $Sr(ClO_4)_2 + K_2SO_4 \rightarrow SrSO_4 + KClO_4$ $Sr(ClO_4)_2 + K_2SO_4 \rightarrow SrSO_4 + 2KClO_4$ ✓
8. $Al + H_2SO_4 \rightarrow Al_2(SO_4)_3 + H_2$ $2Al + 3H_2SO_4 \rightarrow Al_2(SO_4)_3 + 3H_2$ ✓
9. $HNO_3 + H_2S \rightarrow NO + S + H_2O$ $2HNO_3 + 3H_2S \rightarrow 2NO + 3S + 4H_2O$ ✓
10. $Pb(NO_3)_2 + KCl \rightarrow PbCl_2 + KNO_3$ $Pb(NO_3)_2 + 2KCl \rightarrow PbCl_2 + 2KNO_3$ ✓
11. $MgCO_3 + HNO_3 \rightarrow Mg(NO_3)_2 + H_2O + CO_2$
12. $H_2SO_4 + NaOH \rightarrow Na_2SO_4 + H_2O$
13. $SO_2 + HNO_2 \rightarrow H_2SO_4 + NO$
14. $HI + H_2SO_4 \rightarrow H_2O + H_2S + I_2$
15. $HCl + Al(OH)_3 \rightarrow H_2O + AlCl_3$
16. $NaOH + CuSO_4 \rightarrow Na_2SO_4 + Cu(OH)_2$
17. $HF + Ba(NO_3)_2 \rightarrow HNO_3 + BaF_2$
18. $NO_2 + H_2 \rightarrow NH_3 + H_2O$
19. $NH_3 + O_2 \rightarrow NO + H_2O$
20. $HCl + FeCl_2 + H_2O_2 \rightarrow FeCl_3 + H_2O$

Balancing Equations 2

These are best done using the oxidation numbers method

Video links; Balancing Equations Using Oxidation States - Atoms, Electrons, Structure and Bonding #18 https://youtu.be/xQ9th5CpKgo

1. $KBr + H_2SO_4 \rightarrow KHSO_4 + Br_2 + SO_2 + H_2O$
2. $KCl + MnO_2 + H_2SO_4 \rightarrow K_2SO_4 + MnSO_4 + Cl_2 + H_2O$
3. $NaI + H_2SO_4 \rightarrow Na_2SO_4 + I_2 + H_2S + H_2O$
4. $Zn + NO_3^- + H^+ \rightarrow Zn^{2+} + NH_4^+ + H_2O$
5. $HNO_3 + H_3AsO_3 \rightarrow NO + H_3AsO_4 + H_2O$
6. $PbS + H_2O_2 \rightarrow PbSO_4 + H_2O$
7. $Cu + HNO_3 \rightarrow Cu(NO_3)_2 + NO + H_2O$
8. $KIO_3 + KI + H_2SO_4 \rightarrow K_2SO_4 + H_2O + I_2$
9. $Cu + HNO_3 \rightarrow Cu(NO_3)_2 + NO + H_2O$
10. $HNO_3 + I_2 \rightarrow HIO_3 + NO_2 + H_2O$
11. $H_2SO_3 + KMnO_4 \rightarrow K_2SO_4 + MnSO_4 + H_2SO_4 + H_2O$
12. $FeSO_4 + K_2Cr_2O_7 + H_2SO_4 \rightarrow Cr_2(SO_4)_3 + K_2SO_4 + Fe_2(SO_4)_3 + H_2O$
13. $MnSO_4 + NaBiO_3 + H_2SO_4 \rightarrow NaMnO_4 + Bi_2(SO_4)_3 + H_2O + Na_2SO_4$
14. $FeSO_4 + KMnO_4 + H_2SO_4 \rightarrow K_2SO_4 + MnSO_4 + Fe_2(SO_4)_3 + H_2O$
15. $H_2C_2O_4 + KMnO_4 + H_2SO_4 \rightarrow CO_2 + K_2SO_4 + MnSO_4 + H_2O$
16. $MoO_3 + Zn + H_2SO_4 \rightarrow Mo_2O_3 + ZnSO_4 + H_2O$
17. $KMnO_4 + KCl + H_2SO_4 \rightarrow MnSO_4 + K_2SO_4 + H_2O + Cl_2$
18. $KNO_2 + KMnO_4 + H_2SO_4 \rightarrow MnSO_4 + H_2O + KNO_3 + K_2SO_4$
19. $K_2CrO_4 + Na_2SO_3 + HCl \rightarrow KCl + Na_2SO_4 + CrCl_3 + H_2O$
20. $NaOH + Br_2 \rightarrow NaBr + NaBrO_3 + H_2O$

Turning experiments in to balanced symbol equations

For each of the following experiments give the balanced symbol equation

Video links; Writing Balanced Equations from Word Descriptions. https://youtu.be/WtkxGYAuZqU

1. Aluminium and iron (III) oxide are reacted together.
2. Nitrogen and chlorine gas react together.
3. Carbon and chlorine gas react together.
4. Calcium chloride is reacted potassium hydroxide.
5. Tetraphosphorus reacts with chlorine.
6. Ethene completely combusts.
7. Magnesium reacts with carbon dioxide.
8. Hydrogen peroxide decomposes.
9. Ethane completely combusts.
10. Iron (III) oxide can carbon react.
11. Titanium (IV) chloride reacts with magnesium.
12. Phosphine (PH_3) is reacted with oxygen.
13. Phosphane (PH_5) is reacted with oxygen.
14. Copper (II) chloride is reacted with sodium hydroxide.
15. Potassium iodide reacts with lead (II) nitrate.
16. Phosphorus trichloride reacts with water.
17. Propane burns completely.
18. Lead (II) nitrate decomposes.
19. Glucose reacts with oxygen.
20. Ammonia reacts with oxygen.

Organic Chemistry Keywords

You need to learn these, again flashcards to help are available on my website

Addition polymerisation - A long chain formed of repeating units, eg alkenes

Alkane - a hydrocarbon that only has single bonds in it.

General Formula - the simplest algebraic formula for a compound

Empirical Formula - a formula showing the lowest whole number ratios of elements in a compound.

Structural Formula - The minimal amount of detail needed to determine the special arrangement od elements in a compound

Unsaturated - a compounds that has double or triple bonds

Hydrocarbon - a compounds that is made from hydrogen and carbon only

Alkene - a compound that has at least one double bond

Alkyl group - a side chain that has been forms from an alkane by removing a hydrogen

Functional group - the part of an organic compound that is responsible for the properties

Saturated - a compound that only has single bonds

Aromatic - a compound that contains a benzene ring

Alkynes - A compound that has a least one triple bond

Radical - an element or compound that has an unpaired electron

Homologous Series - a set of organic compounds with the same functional group

Displayed formula - This shows that position of all atoms and the bonding between them

Naming Organic Compounds – The Rules

The prefix of the name indicates the number of carbon atoms present in the molecule.

The functional group, and hence the homologous series to which the compound belongs is usually indicated by the suffix of the name.

1. Find the longest carbon - carbon chain (not always straight).
2. Identify the side branches.
3. Circle all the functional groups and identify them.
4. Number the chain so that the branch with the highest priority functional group has the lowest number possible.
5. Di-, tri etc used for more than one branch of same kind.
6. Branches in alphabetical order.
7. Comma's between numbers eg 2,2 or 2,3.
8. Hyphens separate numbers from letters eg 2,2-dimethyl and no gaps between names eg methylpropane

Naming alkanes

Video link; Naming Alkanes Using IUPAC Systematic Nomenclature - Organic Chemistry #1
https://youtu.be/uv7pJsSiq5w

1.

```
      H
      |
  H — C — H
      |
      H
```

a. methane
b. ethane
c. propane
d. butane

2.

```
      H   H   H   H
      |   |   |   |
  H — C — C — C — C — H
      |   |   |   |
      H   H   H   H
```

a. butane
b. propane
c. pentane
d. ethane

3.

```
      H   H   H   H   H
      |   |   |   |   |
  H — C — C — C — C — C — H
      |   |   |   |   |
      H   H   H   H   H
```

a. 2-ethylpropane
b. 1-methylbutane
c. pentane
d. 2-methylpentane

4.

```
          H
          |
      H — C — H
          |
      H       H   H
      |       |   |
  H — C — C — C — C — H
      |   |   |   |
      H   H   H   H
```

a. pentane
b. 2-methylbutane
c. 1-methylbutane
d. 3-methylbutane

5.

a. pentane
b. 2-methylbutane
c. 1-methylbutane
d. 3-methylbutane

6.

a. 2,3-methylbutane
b. 2,2-dimethylbutane
c. 2,3-dimethylpentane
d. 2,3-dimethylbutane

7.

a. 3-ethyl-2-methylbutane
b. 2-ethyl-2-methylbutane
c. 2,3-dimethylpentane
d. 2,3-dimethylbutane

8.

a. 3-methyl-2-ethylhexane
b. 3-ethyl-2-methylhexane
c. 2-ethyl-3-methylhexane
d. 2-methyl-3-ethylhexane

9.

a. 3-ethyl-4-propylhaxane
b. 3-propyl-4-ethylhexane
c. 4-ethyl-3-propylhaxane
d. 3,4-diethlyheptane

10.

a. 3-ethyl-4-methylhexane
b. 3,4-diethylpentane
c. 2,3-diethylpentane
d. 2-ethyl-4-methylhexane

a. 3,4-dimethylhexane
b. 3,4-diethylhexane
c. 4-ethyl-3-methylhexane
d. 4-ethyl-3-methylheptane

11.

a. 3-methylheptane
b. 3,4,4,5-methylheptane
c. 3,4,5-tetramethylheptane
d. 3,4,4,5-tetramethylheptane

12.

a. 4-ethyl-4methylheptane
b. 4-methyl-4ethylheptane
c. 4-methyl-4-propylhexane
d. 3-methyl-3-propylhexane

13.

a. 3,4-dipropylpentane
b. 2,3-dipropylpentane
c. 4,5-diethyl-2-methyloctane
d. 4,5-diethyl-7-methyloctane

14.

a. 7,6,5,4-methylnonane
b. 1,2,3,4,5,6,7-heptamethylheptane
c. 1,2,3,4,5,6,7-methylheptane
d. 3,4,5,6,7-pentamethylnonane

15.

16.

a. 3- bromopropane
b. bromopropane
c. 1-bromopropane
d. 2- bromopropane

17.

a. 3-bromo-1-flourobutane
b. 1-flouro-3-bromorbutane
c. 2-bromo-4-flurobutnae
d. 4-fluor-2-bromobutane

18.

a. 2-bromo-4-chloro-3-fluropentane
b. 2-bromo-3-fluropentane
c. 4-chloro-3-fluropentane
d. 2-bromo-4-chloropentane

19.

a. 2-bromo-3-methylpentane
b. 2,2-dibromo-3-methylpentane
c. 3-methyl 2,2-dibromopentane
d. 4,4-dibromo-3-methylpentane

20.

a. 2,4,7-triflouro-6,7-dichloro-4,6-diethyl-3,5-dibromoctane

b. 2,5,7-triflouro-2,3-dichloro-3,5-diethyl-4,6-dibromooctane

c. 3,5-dibromo-6,7-dichloro-4,6-diethyl-2,4,7-triflourooctane

d. 4,6-dibromo-2,3-dichloro-3,5-diethyl-2,5,7-triflourooctane

Naming Alkenes

Video link; Naming Alkenes Using IUPAC Systematic Nomenclature - Organic Chemistry #2
https://youtu.be/C-Rt17aLXWQ

1.

a. methene
b. ethene
c. methane
d. ethane

2.

a. prop-1-ene
b. prop-2-ene
c. propane
d. prop-3-ene

3.

a. but-4-ene
b. but-3-ene
c. but-2-ene
d. but-1-ene

4.

a. but-4-ene
b. but-3-ene
c. but-2-ene
d. but-1-ene

a. but-4-ene
b. but-3-ene
c. but-2-ene
d. but-1-ene

5.

a. but-1,3-diene
b. but-1-ene
c. but-2-ene
d. but-3-ene

6.

a. 3-methylbut-2-ene
b. 2-methylbut-2-ene
c. pent-2-ene
d. 2-methylpent-2-ene

7.

a. 3,2-methylbut-2-ene
b. 2,3-dimethylbut-2-ene
c. pent-2-ene
d. 2,3-methylpent-2-ene

8.

a. 3-methylpent-2-ene
b. 1,2-dimethylbut-1-ene
c. 3,4-dimethylbut-3-ene
d. 3-methylpent-3-ene

9.

10.

a. 4-ethyl-5-methylhept-3,5-diene
b. 4,5-diethylhex-3,5-diene
c. 4-ethyl-3-methylhex-2,4-diene
d. 4-ethyl-3-methylhept-2,4-diene

11.

a. 3-methylhex-2,4,5-triene
b. 4-methylhex-1,2,4-triene
c. 1-ethyl-1-methylbut-2,3-diene
d. 4-ethyl-4-methyl-but-1,4-diene

12.

a. 2-ethylbutene
b. 3-methylpent-3,4-diene
c. 3-ethylbut-1,2-diene
d. 3-methylpent-1,2-diene

13.

a. 4-ethyl-3,3-dimethylhex-1,4,5-triene
b. 4,4-diethyl-3-methylhex-1,4,5-triene
c. 4,4-diethyl-3-methylhex-1,2,4-triene
d. 4,4-diethyl-3,3-dimethylhex-1,2,5-triene

14.

a. 3,5,7-trimethylhept-3,5-diene
b. 3,6,7-trimethyloct-1,3,5-triene
c. 2,3,6-trimethylhept-3,5,7-diene
d. 2,3,6-trimethylhept-3,5-diene

a. 6-ethyl-3,4-dimethylhept-2,4,5,6-tetraene
b. 2-ethyl-4,5-dimethylhept-1,2,3,5-tetraene
c. 3,5,6-trimethyloct-2,4,5,6-tetraene
d. 4,5,6-trimethyloct-1,2,3,5-tetraene

15.

a. 3-bromobut-1-ene
b. 2-bromobut-3-ene
c. 2-bromobut-2-ene
d. 3-bromobut-2-ene

16.

a. 1-flouro-2-bromo-3-chloro-4-flourobut-2-ene
b. 2-bromo-3-chloro-diflouorbut-2-ene
c. 3-bromo-2-chloro-1,4-diflouorbut-2-ene
d. 2-bromo-3-chloro-1,4-diflouorbutene

17.

18.

a. 1,1,2-tribomo-4-ethyl-3,5-dimethylhex-1,3,5-triene
b. 1-tribomo-4-ethyl-3-dimethylhex-1-triene
c. 1,1,2-tribomo-4-methyl-3,5-dimethylhex-1,3,5-triene
d. 1,1,2-tribomo-4-methyl-3,5-dimethylhept-1,3,5-triene

a. 1,2,3,4-tetrabromopent-1,4-diene
b. tetrabromopent-1,4-diene
c. 1,2,3,4,5-tetrabromopent-1,4-diene
d. 1,2,3,4-tetrabromopent-1,4-diene

19.

20.

a. 1,2,2,5,6-pentabromo-7-chloro-4-ethyl-3-methylhept-3,5-diene

b. 2,3,6,6,7-pentabromo-1-chloro-4-ethyl-5-methylhept-2,4-diene

c. pentabromochloroethylmethylhept-3,5-diene

d. 2,3,6,7-pentabromo-1-chloro-4-ethylhept-2,4-diene

Skeletal formula

Video link; Skeletal Formula - Organic Chemistry #6 https://youtu.be/yiuhhkO2QzY

1.

a. methane
b. ethene
c. ethane
d. propane

2.

a. propane
b. methane
c. ethane
d. ethene

3.

a. butane
b. propane
c. hexane
d. pentane

4.

a. 4-methylpentane
b. methylbutane
c. 2-methylpentane
d. 2-methylbutane

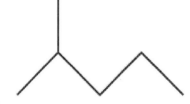

5.

a. pentane
b. 2,4-dimethylbutane
c. 2,4-dimethylpentane
d. 2,4-dimethylhaxane

6.

a. 4-bromo-2-methylheptane
b. 4-bromomethyl-2-methylheptane
c. 4-bromomethyl-2-methylpentane
d. 4-bromomethyl-2-methylhexane

7.

a. 4-ethyl-6-methylheptane
b. 4-ethyl-2-methylheptane
c. 4-ethyl-2-methylhexane
d. -ethyl-6-methylhexane

8.

a. 1,2,3,4,5,6,7,8-hexamethyloctane
b. Tetradecane
c. 2,3,4,5,6,7-hexamethyloctane
d. 2,3,4,5,6,7-methyloctane

9.

a. 2,4,6-tribromo-3,5,7-trichlorooctane
b. 2,3,4,5,6,7-tribromotrichlorooctane
c. 2,4,6-tribromo-3,5,7-trichlorohexane
d. 2,4,6,8-tribromo-1,3,5,7-trichlorohexane

10.

a. pentane
b. pent-3-ene
c. pent-2-ene
d. pent-1-ene

11.

a. hexene
b. hex-1,4-diene
c. hex-2,5-diene
d. pent-1,4-diene

12.

a. 1,3-dicholohex-2,5-diene
b. 3,6-dicholohex-1,4-diene
c. 1,3-dicholopent-1,4-diene
d. 3,5-dicholopent-1,4-diene

13.

a. 3,4-dimethylhex-2,5-diene
b. 4-methylhex-1,4-diene
c. 3,4-diethylhex-2,5-diene
d. 3,4-dimethylhex-1,4-diene

14.

a. 2,3-dimethylhex-1,4-diene
b. 4,5-diemthylhept-2,5-diene
c. 3,4-dimethylhex-1,4-diene
d. 3,4-diemthylhept-2,5-diene

15.

a. 5-bromo-4-ethylhept-2,5-diene
b. 3-bromo-4-ethylhept-2,5-diene
c. 3-bromo-4-methylhept-2,5-diene
d. 3-bromomethyl-4-ethylhept-2,5-diene

16.

a. 3-bromo-1-chloro-4-ethyl-2,5-dimethylhept-2,5-diene
b. 1-chloro-3-bromo-4-ethyl-2,5-dimethylhept-2,5-diene
c. 5-bromo-7-chloro-4-ethyl-3,6-dimethylhept-2,5-diene
d. 5-bromo-8-chloro-4-ethyl-3,6-dimethyloct-2,5-diene

17.

a. 4-bromo-1-chloro-5-ethlyoct-3,7-diene
b. 5-bromo-7-chloro-4-ethlyhept-2,5-diene
c. 3-bromo-1-chloro-4-ethlyhept-2,5-diene
d. 3-bromo-1-chloro-4-ethlyhex-2,5-diene

18.

a. 2-bromo-3-chloro-4-ethylhept-4,6-diene
b. 6-bromo-5-chloro-4-ethylhept-1,3-diene
c. 6-bromo-5-chloro-4-ethylhex-1,3-diene
d. 2-bromo-3-chloro-4-ethylhex-4,6-diene

19.

a. 4-ethyl-2,3,3-trimethlyheptane
b. Bob
c. 4-propyl-2,3,3-trimethlyhexane
d. 4-ethyl-2,3,3methlyheptane

20.

a. 8-chloro-3,9,10-triethyl-5-methyldodec-7,10-diene
b. 5-chloro-3,4,10-triethyl-8-methyldodec-2,5-diene
c. 5-chloro-3,4,10-ethyl-8-methyldec-2,5-ene
d. 8-chloro-3,9,10-triethyl-5-methyldec-7,10-diene

Answers

Atomic structure

1. b
2. a
3. a
4. a
5. b
6. b
7. c
8. a
9. c
10. b
11. b
12. a
13. d
14. c
15. a
16. c
17. a
18. b
19. b
20. D

Properties of ionic compounds

1. b
2. c
3. c
4. c
5. d
6. d
7. c
8. b

9. d

10. c

11. c

12. c

13. b

14. c

15. d

Covalent bonding

1. c

2. b

3. a

4. b

5. b

6. d

7. d

8. a

9. b

10. c

11. c

12. a

13. B and d

14. b

15. a

16. a

17. b

18. a

19. a

20. C

Formula of Ionic Compounds

1. AgI

2. MgI$_2$

3. LiI

4. PbI_2

5. CuI_2

6. $FeBr_3$

7. $FeBr_2$

8. $BaBr_2$

9. $SrBr_2$

10. $SrCl_2$

11. $CuCl_2$

12. $FeCl_2$

13. $CaCl_2$

14. $LiCl_2$

15. $BaCl_2$

16. Na_2O

17. K_2O

18. ZnO

19. Al_2O_3

20. SrO

21. Cu_2O

22. CuO

23. Fe_2O_3

24. FeO

25. Cr_2O_3

26. $FeCO_3$

27. $(NH_4)_2CO_3$

28. $CuCO_3$

29. $PbCO_3$

30. Na_2CO_3

31. $MgCO_3$

32. $FeCO_3$

33. $BaCO_3$

34. $KHCO_3$

35. $Sr(HCO_3)_2$

36. $LiHCO_3$

37. NH_4HCO_3

38. $NaHCO_3$

39. $Mg(HCO_3)_2$

40. $(NH_4)_2S$

41. FeS

42. Al_2S_3

43. $Fe_2(SO_4)_3$

44. $FeSO_4$

45. $PbSO_4$

46. $Al_2(SO_4)_3$

47. $ZnSO_4$

48. $BaSO_4$

49. $(NH_4)_2SO_4$

50. $MgSO_4$

51. Li_2SO_4

52. $Mg(OH)_2$

53. $Al(OH)_3$

54. KOH

55. NH_4OH

56. $Ba(OH)_2$

57. LiOH

58. $Ca(OH)_2$

59. $Sr(OH)_2$

60. $Al(NO_3)_3$

61. NH_4NO_3

62. $Pb(NO_3)_2$

63. $NaNO_2$

64. Li_3N

65. Mg_3N_2

Oxidation numbers

1. a
2. b
3. a
4. a
5. c
6. c
7. c
8. c
9. d
10. d

11. c
12. d
13. b
14. a
15. a
16. c
17. b
18. c
19. d
20. A

Balancing Equations 1

These are best done by trial and error

1. $2Mg + 2HIO_3 \rightarrow 2Mg(IO_3) + H_2$
2. $BaCl_2 + Na_2SO_4 \rightarrow 2NaCl + BaSO_4$
3. $NaI + 3HOCl \rightarrow NaIO_3 + 3HCl$
4. $4Al + 3MnO_2 \rightarrow 2Al_2O_3 + 3Mn$
5. $Ba(OH)_2 + H_2SO_4 \rightarrow BaSO_4 + 2H_2O$
6. $K_2CO_3 + 2AgNO_3 \rightarrow 2KNO_3 + Ag_2CO_3$
7. $Sr(ClO_4)_2 + K_2SO_4 \rightarrow SrSO_4 + 2KClO_4$
8. $2Al + 3H_2SO_4 \rightarrow Al_2(SO_4)_3 + 3H_2$
9. $2HNO_3 + 3H_2S \rightarrow 2NO + 3S + 4H_2O$
10. $Pb(NO_3)_2 + 2KCl \rightarrow PbCl_2 + 2KNO_3$
11. $MgCO_3 + 2HNO_3 \rightarrow Mg(NO_3)_2 + H_2O + CO_2$
12. $H_2SO_4 + 2NaOH \rightarrow Na_2SO_4 + 2H_2O$
13. $SO_2 + 2HNO_2 \rightarrow H_2SO_4 + 2NO$
14. $8HI + H_2SO_4 \rightarrow 4H_2O + H_2S + 4I_2$
15. $3HCl + Al(OH)_3 \rightarrow 3H_2O + AlCl_3$
16. $2NaOH + CuSO_4 \rightarrow Na_2SO_4 + Cu(OH)_2$
17. $2HF + Ba(NO_3)_2 \rightarrow 2HNO_3 + BaF_2$
18. $2NO_2 + 7H_2 \rightarrow 2NH_3 + 4H_2O$
19. $4NH_3 + 5O_2 \rightarrow 4NO + 6H_2O$
20. $2HCl + 2FeCl_2 + H_2O_2 \rightarrow 2FeCl_3 + 2H_2O$

Balancing Equations 2

These are best done using the oxidation numbers method

1. $2KBr + 3H_2SO_4 \rightarrow 2KHSO_4 + Br_2 + SO_2 + 2H_2O$
2. $2KCl + MnO_2 + 2H_2SO_4 \rightarrow K_2SO_4 + MnSO_4 + Cl_2 + 2H_2O$
3. $8NaI + 5H_2SO_4 \rightarrow 4Na_2SO_4 + 4I_2 + H_2S + 4H_2O$
4. $4Zn + NO_3^- + 10H^+ \rightarrow 4Zn^{2+} + NH_4^+ + 3H_2O$
5. $2HNO_3 + 3H_3AsO_3 \rightarrow 2NO + 3H_3AsO_4 + H_2O$
6. $PbS + 4H_2O_2 \rightarrow PbSO_4 + 4H_2O$
7. $3Cu + 8HNO_3 \rightarrow 3Cu(NO_3)_2 + 2NO + 4H_2O$
8. $KIO_3 + 5KI + 3H_2SO_4 \rightarrow 3K_2SO_4 + 3H_2O + 3I_2$
9. $3Cu + 8HNO_3 \rightarrow 3Cu(NO_3)_2 + 2NO + 4H_2O$
10. $10HNO_3 + I_2 \rightarrow 2HIO_3 + 10NO_2 + 4H_2O$
11. $5H_2SO_3 + 2KMnO_4 \rightarrow K_2SO_4 + 2MnSO_4 + 2H_2SO_4 + 3H_2O$
12. $6FeSO_4 + K_2Cr_2O_7 + 7H_2SO_4 \rightarrow Cr_2(SO_4)_3 + K_2SO_4 + 3Fe_2(SO_4)_3 + 7H_2O$
13. $4MnSO_4 + 10NaBiO_3 + 14H_2SO_4 \rightarrow 4NaMnO_4 + 5Bi_2(SO_4)_3 + 14H_2O + 3Na_2SO_4$
14. $10FeSO_4 + 2KMnO_4 + 8H_2SO_4 \rightarrow K_2SO_4 + 2MnSO_4 + 5Fe_2(SO_4)_3 + 8H_2O$
15. $5H_2C_2O_4 + 2KMnO_4 + 3H_2SO_4 \rightarrow 10CO_2 + K_2SO_4 + 2MnSO_4 + 8H_2O$
16. $2MoO_3 + 3Zn + 3H_2SO_4 \rightarrow Mo_2O_3 + 3ZnSO_4 + 3H_2O$
17. $2KMnO_4 + 10KCl + 8H_2SO_4 \rightarrow 2MnSO_4 + 6K_2SO_4 + 8H_2O + 5Cl_2$
18. $5KNO_2 + 2KMnO_4 + 3H_2SO_4 \rightarrow 2MnSO_4 + 3H_2O + 5KNO_3 + K_2SO_4$
19. $2K_2CrO_4 + 3Na_2SO_3 + 10HCl \rightarrow 4KCl + 3Na_2SO_4 + 2CrCl_3 + 5H_2O$
20. $6NaOH + 3Br_2 \rightarrow 5NaBr + NaBrO_3 + 3H_2O$

Turning experiments in to balanced symbol equations

1. $Fe_2O_3 + 2Al \rightarrow 2Fe + Al_2O_3$
2. $N_2 + 3Cl_2 \rightarrow 2NCl_3$
3. $C + 2Cl_2 \rightarrow CCl_4$
4. $CaCl_2 + 2KOH \rightarrow Ca(OH)_2 + 2KCl$
5. $P_4 + 6Cl_2 \rightarrow 4PCl_3$
6. $C_2H_4 + 3O_2 \rightarrow 2CO_2 + 2H_2O$

7. $2Mg + CO_2 \rightarrow 2MgO + C$
8. $2H_2O_2 \rightarrow 2H_2O + O_2$
9. $2C_2H_6 + 7O_2 \rightarrow 4CO_2 + 6H_2O$
10. $Fe_2O_3 + 3C \rightarrow 2Fe + 3CO$
11. $TiCl_4 + 2Mg \rightarrow 2MgCl_2 + Ti$
12. $2PH_3 + 3O_2 \rightarrow P_2O_3 + 3H_2O$
13. $2PH_5 + 5O_2 \rightarrow P_2O_5 + 5H_2O$
14. $CuCl_2 + 2NaOH \rightarrow Cu(OH)_2 + 2NaCl$
15. $2KI + Pb(NO_3)_2 \rightarrow 2KNO_3 + PbI_2$
16. $PCl_3 + 3H_2O \rightarrow P(OH)_3 + 3HCl$
17. $C_3H_8 + 5O_2 \rightarrow 5CO_2 + 4H_2O$
18. $2Pb(NO_3)_2 \rightarrow 2PbO + 4NO_2 + O_2$
19. $C_6H_{12}O_6 + 6O_2 \rightarrow 6H_2O + 6CO_2$
20. $4NH_3 + 5O_2 \rightarrow 4NO + 6H_2O$

Naming alkanes

1. a
2. a
3. c
4. b
5. b
6. d
7. c
8. b
9. d
10. a
11. c
12. d
13. a
14. c
15. d
16. c
17. a
18. a
19. b

20. D

Naming alkenes

Answer key

1. b
2. a
3. d
4. c
5. d
6. a
7. b
8. b
9. a
10. d
11. b
12. d
13. a
14. b
15. d
16. a
17. c
18. a
19. d
20. B

Skeletal formula

1. c
2. a
3. d
4. c
5. c
6. a
7. b
8. c
9. a

10. c
11. b
12. c
13. d
14. d
15. b
16. a
17. c
18. b
19. a
20. B

30320835R00033

Printed in Poland
by Amazon Fulfillment
Poland Sp. z o.o., Wrocław